PATHWAYS TO THE GARDEN

PATHWAYS TO THE GARDEN

Contemporary Insights for the Sufi Path

SHAYKH FADHLALLA HAERI

Zahra Publications

Published by Zahra Publications
www.shaykhfadhlallahaeri.com
www.zahrapublications.pub

© Shaykh Fadhlalla Haeri, 2024

All rights reserved. Except for brief quotations in critical articles or reviews, no part of this book may be reproduced in any manner without prior written permission from Zahra Publications.

Copying and redistribution of this book is strictly prohibited.
Designed and typeset in South Africa by Quintessence Publishing

Set in 11 points on 13 points, Garamond
Printed and bound by Lightning Source

ISBN (Printed Version) — Paperback: 978-1-928329-44-2

TABLE OF CONTENTS

Introduction --- 1

What is our purpose? -- 4

Who am I, and what am I not? ------------------------------- 6

Is inner peace and contentment possible in today's time? ------ 10

How do we break habits and overcome desires? --------------- 14

How can we transcend our obsession with benefits and outcomes? --- 18

How does one reconcile the light of the spirit with the shadow of the self? -- 22

What is the ultimate human quest? ------------------------- 26

What is the role of illusion in life? --------------------------- 30

How does one see things as they truly are? ------------------ 34

How does one have a clear head and a pure heart? ------------ 38

What are the main obstacles to awakening to the inner truth? -- 42

How can one attain a clear mind and live contentedly in a disturbed world? --- 46

What is the prescription to stop the mind? ------------------ 50

What role does religion play in awakening and illumination? --- 54

How can we live in the moment fully? --- 58

How can one attain pure awareness? --- 62

How can we be prepared, ready and cheerful about death? --- 66

What does it mean to die before you die? --- 70

How does one take reference from the Higher without a visible outer authority? --- 74

What is the role of fear and hope in awakening? --- 78

What is the role of knowledge in awakening? --- 82

What is the importance of balance and how do we attain it? --- 86

What are the qualities of the 'middle people'? --- 90

What does it mean to empty our mind and purify our heart? --- 94

Why are we driven towards achievement and success? --- 98

What is the truth about karma? --- 102

What is Wahm and Khayal? --- 106

What is Fana and Baqa? --- 110

What is Tawakkul? --- 114

What is the reason and purpose of worship? --- 118

What are the pitfalls on the path towards Oneness? ---------- 122

What does it mean to witness perfection? ------------------- 126

What is our ultimate destiny? ----------------------------- 130

INTRODUCTION

Cosmic Light is boundless, eternal and contains the entire universe. Throughout human history, irrespective of religious orientation or culture, humans have sought after the eternal truth of this Reality. A sage like Shaykh Saʿd ud-Dīn Mahmūd Shabistārī was able to convey important aspects of this in a universal light. One of his books of poetry written in 1317 CE, Gulshan-e Rāz or 'The Secret Garden', offers guiding insights into the realities of the Sufi path.

Not much is known about the life of Shaykh Shabistārī, who was born around 1250 CE in Shabistār, near Tabrīz in Iran, during the turbulent times of the Mongol invasions. He wrote two popular poetry collections and at least one treatise. 'The Secret Garden', one of his two works of mystical poetry, had been composed in response to questions on metaphysics sent to him by a contemporary Sufi Master, Shaykh Rukn ad-Dīn Husaynī Harawī, himself a renowned Sufi master from Azerbaijan. Adeptly referring to the imagery used by previous Sufi poets, Shabistārī's work feeds into the tradition of Sufi language, as he elaborates on realities of the journey of awakening. Shabistārī's penetrating answers and symbolic expositions cover critical facets on awakening to the human soul and the doctrine of the 'Unity of Being' as represented in the work of Ibn 'Arabī, among others. His exposition reveals the interconnectedness of reason, revelation and unveiling in the symbolic garden. Shabistārī's answers to the critical questions about the nature of humanity and the Divine may propel us along the ladder of consciousness towards the eternal supreme light of existence.

In my experience and understanding, the conditioned consciousness of human beings has within it a drive towards higher consciousness and intelligence. Throughout our history, this appears in diverse ways and forms, cloaked within the culture of the time. With the rise in intelligence and education, today's people can easily understand duality and the quest for unity without it being too esoteric.

Young people today can also appreciate the truth that our existence has emerged from a mysterious, unific source and is sustained by it and will unify with it. Every one of us is challenged by the mystery of time, which is ever-changing and yet constant, and the unique gift of life.

Introduction

All quests and teachings lead to the realisation that the soul, or essence of life, is eternal and radiates from time and its flow within space. We are obsessed with that which is eternal and boundless – the divine soul or spirit within the heart.

I have tried to make a modern translation of 'The Secret Garden' available and on several occasions I had visions of Shaykh Shabistārī and others like Ibn 'Arabī, Mulla Sadrā, Shaykh Rūzbehān Bāqli and Ibn 'Atā' Allah al-Iskandarī, in which they would look at me with quizzical expressions as if to say, 'You do not need to redo the classical works of past masters, for they were for the people of that time. Truth is eternal and appears appropriately at every point in time. Now you need to answer the questions for your time.'

It is in that spirit which I hope to address these questions in this book.

Shaykh Fadhlalla Haeri

South Africa, 2024

WHAT IS OUR PURPOSE?

Human life on earth demands participation and interaction to experience a better outcome within our consciousness of dualities, some of our participative efforts are attractive and useful, while others are detrimental. Our earthly life drives us to climb along the ladder of higher intelligence through trial and error. This is the real evolutionary progress.

Our purpose on earth is to prepare for the highest stage of consciousness which comes after the removal of the body and the mind. Higher quality life only begins after death. To realise this purpose we need to move our focus from the numerous shadows emanating from the one light from our own heart, spirit or soul towards the constant inner light. When we die, all the shadows disappear and only the light of the soul remains.

We have to practice shadow disappearance and emergence of pure inner light.

Once you truly discover the truth that the source of life within you is Divine and boundless, then the fear of death will abate and concerns for any loss will also disappear. The old and false identity of the ego-self is now the effulgent soul.

> *Prepare yourself for the highest consciousness.*

51:56 *I created jinn and mankind only to worship Me:*

23:1 *Prosperous are the believers.*

67:2 *Who created death and life that He may try you – which of you is best in deeds; and He is the Mighty, the Forgiving.*

WHO AM I, AND WHAT AM I NOT?

It is natural for intelligent human beings to question their real nature, the reasons for their actions and state of being, and to reflect upon what to do and what not to do.

Who am I? Why do we change or reverse our value systems? Why do we long to leave normal consciousness behind and embrace deep sleep?

We learn a lot by realising who we are not. I am not just the pursuer of success or wealth and power, although in a list of priorities of what I desire, power and wealth may appear right on top. Ultimately the main drive in my life is to preserve and prolong life. That is the most valuable entity there is — life — which causes my experiences of life itself.

Throughout the millennia, a few individuals have touched supreme consciousness to assist us by showing that duality in life enables us to understand the timeless eternal nature of life itself, as well as the more defined and confined nature of the animal life that we harbour. The outcome of these spiritual inspirations is that the human being is composed of two entities: one is a divine eternal light which carries life with it, and the other one is an animal that enables it to function in an intermediate and transitional state on earth, where it participates in the pursuit of what is considered to be good for it, like nourishment, rest, safety, security and personal and social harmony.

Ultimately, the so-called 'I' emanates from the constant light of life, which enables it to experience all the various shadows and flavours of likes and dislikes, acceptances and rejections, and other dualities.

It is in our nature to seek an inner state that is ever-constant for that is where your soul resides.

The real 'I' is a constant soul with a heavenly nature undergoing an earthly exposure. Durability will further define the perception. You may be a disappointed friend or an anxious

Who am I, and what am I not?

parent or a pursuer of material success, but all of these roles have a limited durability, until you end up at your origin, pure and eternal.

Life is not constrained by space or time. But emerges within space and time, like a flame it emerges and then subsides.

The fundamental 'I' is the experiencer with the evaluation that goes with it. The changing or prevailing experience is taken as an aspect of personality or character. Nothing is ever constant like change itself. The Source of cognisance, experience or the so-called 'I' is ever constant. That is the nature of the soul within the heart. The outer appearance always changes, whereas the inner source is constant.

The real 'I' has the potential to experience and respond to events and stimuli. The so-called 'I' accepts, rejects, or suffers. The real me is inseparable from that which is eternally and boundlessly present: life.

15:29 And when I have formed him fully and breathed into him of My spirit, fall down before him in prostration! '

21:35 Every soul shall taste death. We put you to the test, with evil and good, as an ordeal, and to Us you shall return.

67:2 Who created death and life that He may try you – which of you is best in deeds; and He is the Mighty, the Forgiving,

IS INNER PEACE AND CONTENTMENT POSSIBLE IN TODAY'S TIME?

The human drive for peace and contentment is constant in all situations, including during manmade or natural disasters. Peace and contentment are the ultimate hopes and objectives for intelligent living beings, irrespective of place, culture or time.

Life is experienced through movement or change within time and that is disturbance and agitation and whatever we experience has disturbed peace, but it may be desirable for other reasons. If durable peace, tranquillity and perfect presence is desired, then the ego-self needs to be still and inert.

Peace is the foundation state from which existence emerges. Peace is a field of energy that has not been affected by our emotions, agitation, needs or anxiety. Peace exudes tranquillity and timelessness.

The power of the sacred soul is most experienced with peace and stillness. With the stillness of the ego-self and through peace, the divine power of the soul is naturally experienced and appreciated.

> *Peace is more accessible when the ego-self is less dominant.*

Is inner peace and contentment possible in today's time?

89:27-30 O self at peace! Return to your Lord, well pleased, well pleasing, And enter among My worshippers, and enter My Garden!

13:28 Those who have faith and whose hearts find peace in the remembrance of Allah – truly it is in the remembrance of Allah that hearts find peace.

8:10 Allah did not bring this about except as glad tidings, and so that your hearts might be calmed thereby. Victory comes only from Allah; Allah is Almighty, All-Wise.

How do we break habits and overcome desires?

Habits are formed naturally due to our desire for continuity in the flow of life. Desirable habits serve the soul within the heart and undesirable habits are ego-self enhancers. With wisdom we choose the habits that enable the soul to shine and lead instead of falling into the darkness of the lower self.

We can break habits by replacing them with new, more elevated habits and actions. Replacing old habits with better ones moves us towards higher consciousness.

We naturally repeat what we like and avoid what we don't like. But what you may desire today may be something you will avoid tomorrow. A good quality life is based on a flexible attitude that is connected to the moment. Willingness to change simple daily routines regarding, for example, food, work or relationships is healthy. Changing the type of food you eat, or the time of day you eat, or sleeping in different locations will cultivate flexibility. Subjecting yourself to situations that are outside of your routine can bring freshness in your interaction with the outer world.

Habits give the illusion of continuity due to their repetitiveness. Desires are natural drives towards what we imagine will give us reliable contentment.

Overcoming desires comes with experience and wisdom. Eventually you will realise that all earthly events are temporary anyway; the zest and drive you had for those desires will fall away, and your interest in them will dissipate. With each new era in your life, it will become easier to lose interest in most of your previous desires. A five year old longs for a tricycle, while a seventy year old prefers safety and ease.

How do we break habits and overcome desires?

2:170 But when it is said to them, 'Follow the message that Allah has sent down,' they answer, 'We follow the ways of our fathers.' What! Even though their fathers understood nothing and were not guided?

3:145 A self cannot die save by Allah's leave, at a date to be determined. Whoso desires the reward of this world, We shall give him thereof, and whoso desires the reward of the other world We shall give him thereof. We shall recompense those who give thanks.

5:48 We sent down to you the book with the truth, confirming the book that came before it and with final authority over them; so judge between them according to what Allah has sent down. Do not follow their whims, which deviate from the truth that has come to you. We have assigned a law and a path to each of you. If Allah had so willed, He would have made you one community, but He wanted to test you through that which He has given you, so race to do good: you will all return to Allah and He will make clear to you the matters you differed about.

87:14 He indeed shall be successful who purifies himself.

How can we transcend our obsession with benefits and outcomes?

Within conditioned consciousness lies the natural drive to succeed and achieve beneficial outcomes. Transcendence means a different consciousness to that of gain and loss. When you are able to stop aspirations and ambitions in the outer world, you are at the boundary of a higher level of consciousness. The drive is constant and without an end.

We normally operate in one of two modes: neutral or non-participating, and participating. When we are participating in life it helps us to grow in intelligence and consciousness, but in this mode there isn't any possibility of transcendence. Only when we are neutral, or 'in the moment', and not pre-occupied with our thoughts, desires or projects, we can enquire and search for source and origin. However, looking for the eternal light of the cosmic divine does not diminish the engagement with the human role.

Human consciousness links cosmic boundless consciousness with limited earthly consciousness. As such we are "middle people." These two zones link, but do not mingle.

Transcendence means accessing a different consciousness to that of achieving outcomes.

How can we transcend our obsession with benefits and outcomes?

70:19 Man was truly created anxious.

35:18 No soul burdened can carry the burden of another. If a soul heavy-laden calls for help with its load, not a speck of it shall be carried, not even by a relative. You are to warn those who fear their Lord in the realm of the Unseen, and who perform the prayer. Whoso is pure in soul, his purity rebounds to his own benefit, and to Allah is the final destination.

87:14 He indeed shall be successful who purifies himself.

How does one reconcile the light of the spirit with the shadow of the self?

The shadow of the ego-self stems from the emergence of the light of the soul which radiates life.

At all times you are two. One is constant and unchanging within space and time. That is the soul, a reflection of the Divine, the Ever-Living. The other is its shadow, or the ego-self, carrying a trace of the light of the soul. It is given a temporary reality through your conditioned consciousness and is also the author of a changing biography.

Many memories link the present moment with traces of past events and thus disclose values of importance at that stage in life. Higher consciousness is like a beam of light revealing shadows and images which have made an impact at that state of consciousness.

Humanity is the earthly materialisation of the divine spirit within. It is a creature that has evolved over billions of years, brought to life by the mysterious power of the soul or spirit. If you regard the human as a divine spirit, then you grasp the extent of distractions and lack of accountability and honesty in most of human intentions and actions.

Faith and trust in the perfection of creation motivate us to realise the ever-present source and origin of all.

If you are able to put yourself, your body, mind, heart and emotions, in the other person's position, then you understand their behaviour and values. You will behave exactly as they did, good or bad, acceptable or not. It is only then that you are able to forgive anyone anything. But you have to put yourself entirely into that position in order to liberate yourself from

How does one reconcile the light of the spirit with the shadow of the self?

judgment. The human attempt to be fair and just is an attempt to understand "the other."

Pathways to the Garden

91:7 by the self and how He formed it

91:8 and inspired it to its rebellion and piety!

91:9 He will indeed be successful who purifies it,

56:62 You know all about the first creation – will you not remember and reflect?

WHAT IS THE ULTIMATE HUMAN QUEST?

The natural human drive is towards higher consciousness from a position of safety, security. We need to participate in the dynamics of life by using our faculties to receive signals and transmit our responses as best we can. Excelling in our intentions and actions causes intelligence to rise towards its origin and spiritual roots.

Our human objective is to realise that in essence we are all the same, even if we vary in outer and inner qualities. It is necessary for our well-being to act with fairness, kindness and accountability, to be tranquil and present in the moment irrespective of the situation we are in.

What is the ultimate quest? To have no quest. The ultimate quest is to be so content that the issue of objective no longer arises. Once there, there is no victorious one except The One.

However, once we have been successful in one quest, there will invariably be another. There will always be a drive for something else. Yet we aspire to be content at all times, to have no needs, desires, fears or sorrows. We are engulfed within the field of dualities and are challenged to choose that which causes the least disturbance and suffering. By reference to the zone of oneness we rise on the ladder of intelligence towards its cosmic source – the divine.

> *To witness the temporary and changing times whilst secure in the eternal nature of life itself.*

What is the ultimate human quest?

84:6 you humans, toiling laboriously towards your Lord, will meet Him:

70:19 Man was truly created anxious.

70:20 Whenever misfortune touches him, he is filled with self-pity.

WHAT IS THE ROLE OF ILLUSION IN LIFE?

Truth, Reality, or Divine light is immense and unique and can only be seen from behind with veils and covers that reduce its intensity. It is just like trying to view the sun: you need a shield or dark glass to look at it. Much of what we experience is modified through the filters of perceptions and conditioning. Whatever you experience is a modified version of its reality.

The so-called human self is a reflection or shadow of the soul, whose nature is eternal, constant and divine. What a three-year-old aspires for, cries for, or is frightened by, is very different from what a nine year old may experience. The personal filters of consciousness are being developed to provide an appropriate perspective for our experiences. A three-year-old may experience the loss of a toy as catastrophic, and a sixty-year-old grandfather, reassuringly holds the little child to calm him down. Perspective brings stability and understanding

A time may come in the personal journey towards awakening that one will know that all worldly events are metaphors of the dynamics that play out between desirables and undesirables, none of which are sustainable or durable. A being at that level of consciousness tries to minimise what is upsetting, but equally will not grieve excessively for any loss, because it occurs in time, and time is always transient. The experience of loss always weighs heavier than gain, and the ultimate loss is not having experienced eternal and boundless consciousness, which connects with the divine cosmic light.

> *Our conditioned consciousness can function within the field of dualities and other illusions.*

We are equipped with a consciousness that provides the movie screen, the projector and the moving images, as well as the viewer. These experiences are illusions that appear real at the time. While you are having a nightmare, your response

What is the role of illusion in life?

is that of horror, and you are relieved when you wake up to a more durable awakened state.

Once you realise that all your experiences are illusory and changeable and there is no constancy or durability in emotions or thoughts, then you will not give them the credence and importance you had once afforded them. Truth radiates from the light that provides the experience of life itself.

57:9 It is He who has sent down clear revelations to His Servant, so that He may bring you from the depths of darkness into light; Allah is truly kind and merciful to you.

3:7 It is He Who sent down the Book upon you. In it are verses precise in meaning, these are the very heart of the Book. Others are ambiguous. Those in whose heart is waywardness pursue what is ambiguous therein, seeking discord and seeking to unravel its interpretation. But none knows its interpretation save Allah, while those deeply rooted in knowledge say: 'We believe in it. All is from our Lord.' Yet none remembers save those possessed of the kernel.

2:155 We shall be testing you with some fear and famine, with loss of wealth, lives and crops: But give glad tidings to the patient.

How does one see things as they truly are?

Whatever we think of, intend, or act upon has its root in the divine soul within. To understand what reality is, we need to understand its origin or soul. Every aspect of existence, even the most temporary, carries with it a touch of the real, which is eternal, stable and ever-present.

Whatever exists in this world of dualities has been touched by the original light of the cosmic soul from which it has emerged. Once anything is born into our consciousness, it is within duality. The illusion of durability makes what is transient seem constant. What we seek is permanency. For that reason, one wants a relationship that is everlasting, stability that is always there, and wealth or value that will not erode.

Reality appears in numerous different grades of durability and what is considered important is most durable for us. The loss of sleep for a night or two is obviously considered as less important than the loss of breathing for a minute or two. An hour of parental disapproval is far more tolerable than the absence of a parent for weeks. It is the connectedness and the continuity of events or experiences that give us the illusion of reliability and stability in the world of constant change. To see things as they are, perspective with appropriate context is needed. However, observing it from the changing perspective, one will see things from a survivalist point of view and continue the drive for human survival. The ultimate reference point is the ever-continuing life which emanates from the cosmic source. Once the power

> *Durable reality illumines temporary occurrences within time and space and the less one is engaged with these, the closer one is to the Real.*

of life touches any creature, it drives it towards values defined as beneficial, good or desirable.

84:6 you humans, toiling laboriously towards your Lord, will meet Him:

15:99 and worship your Lord until Certainty comes to you.

102:5 No indeed! If only you knew for certain.

102:7 you will see it with the eye of certainty.

How does one have a clear head and a pure heart?

In today's culture, we generally associate matters of mind, reason and rationality with the head; and those of higher consciousness and soul, with the heart. The head deals with the duality of earthly existence, whereas the heart has within it the soul or spirit, the source and cause of life itself, which is both heavenly and earthly. The soul belongs to a higher dimension of consciousness, but it enables the normal day to day consciousness to function as a human.

The mind, or head, has to do with the balance of the inner and outer worlds. Your head or reason connects the individual entity with habits, expectations, and the definition of well-being of the body and mind. The mind reveals the relationship between your inner state and the environment. It seeks optimum safety and stability and connects all possibilities with your position in the world. Your mind is the connector between your heavenly soul and your human life on earth. For a fulfilled life on earth you need a healthy and tranquil mid.

The heart is the home of the source of life, which is the ruh (soul or spirit). The heart is home to your soul or spirit and it gives rise to your experience of life.

A clear heart is not tainted by expectations, anxieties, fears, wants and disappointments. This means that the light from the heart itself is not blurred by fears, sorrows, anticipations and hopes. All of these distractions prevent us from seeing things as they really are or how we want them to be.

> *Reason and rationality bring balance and continuity to our human state, whereas the heart or soul connects us to the absolute origin and source of existence.*

How does one have a clear head and a pure heart?

The ego-self is the main factor that affects the clarity of vision. A clear heart shines bright.

A wise person benefits from the appropriate signals from different sources and can differentiate light from shadow.

The heart is the metaphorical centre of one's life. Negative emotions like fear, jealousy, anxiety and hatred can all tarnish the heart, thereby reducing the clear light transmitted from the ruh. The light of the soul then becomes dim and cannot provide sufficient energies for the human being to live a wholesome life.

The heart is where emotions reside. They can cause a lot of confusion, especially when they are not dealt with appropriately.

The head draws the energy from the heart, but modifies it to the level of earthly consciousness. If the head is to function optimally, it needs to recalibrate with the heart, which is at the highest level of consciousness. Only then the human earthly state is at its best.

56:79 *That only the purified can touch,*

87:14 *He indeed shall be successful who purifies himself.*

What are the main obstacles to awakening to the inner truth?

The nature of duality in our human consciousness is such that the more sublime the pursuit, the more challenging and subtle the path may be. In most cases, the obstacles are natural and cause delays in the realisation of the absolute Light. The most persistent distraction is the shadow of the soul, which brings about the darkness of the lower self and ego.

The nature of the lower self is fickle. It is a weak reflection of its higher source – the soul within. It is also influenced and affected by several other forces such as the autonomic nervous system, which is involved in regulating our heartbeat, breathing, blood pressure and digestion. Up to twenty percent of our nervous system is tied up to that.

One's overall state of health depends on one's overall trust and faith in the Cosmic governance. Truth is the radiating power of eternal reality and can be traced in outer, inner, seen and unknown situations. Another proof of divine presence and dominance.

> *Truth permeates what is both known and unknown inner and outer states.*

What are the main obstacles to awakening to the inner truth?

58:18 On the Day Allah raises them all from the dead, they will swear before Him as they swear before you now, thinking that it will help them. What liars they are!

8:49 When the hypocrites, and those in whose hearts was sickness, said, 'Their religion has deluded them;" but whosoever puts his trust in Allah, surely Allah is All-Mighty, All-Wise.

6:24 See how they lie to themselves! How their fabrication abandoned them!

How can one attain a clear mind and live contentedly in a disturbed world?

The mind busies itself with dualities and the preservation of life on earth. Therefore it is limited and most useful within the clear boundaries of space and time.

The mind is the mediator that connects the highest realties, which are eternal and boundless, with conditioned consciousness and the earthly dualities. It affirms and confirms humanity and as such it may be detracting from Divinity.

For a mind to function efficiently it must focus on its earthly objective with regular reference and calibration with the soul. It needs to interact with the world of dualities and conditioned consciousness while constantly connecting to the universal source.

A healthy, clear mind is necessary for survival and rise in intelligence and consciousness. To shift from conditioned consciousness to higher levels of consciousness, the mind can be a distraction. You need to move into the zone of your own soul and intuitive consciousness where questions of earthly efficiency do not even arise.

> *The mind mediates between the eternal and boundless and the conditioned consciousness or ego-self.*

How can one attain a clear mind and live contentedly in a disturbed world?

3:191 Those who remember Allah standing, sitting, and lying down, who reflect on the creation of the heavens and earth: 'Our Lord! You have not created all this without purpose – You are far above that, so protect us from the torment of the Fire.

6:50 Say: I do not tell you that I possess the treasures of Allah, nor do I know the Unseen. Nor do I tell you I am an angel. I merely follow what is revealed to me. Say: 'Is the blind man the equal of one who sees? Will you not reflect?'

13:16 Say: 'Who is the Lord of the heaven and earth?' Say: 'Allah!' Say: 'So have you taken to yourselves as protectors, instead of Him, such as are powerless to benefit or harm themselves?' Say: 'Is the blind man the equal of one who sees? Or is darkness the equal of light? Or have they fashioned partners to Allah who created something similar to His creation, and so creation became a matter that perplexed them?' Say: 'Allah is the Creator of all things; He is One, Overpowering.'

11:24 The likeness of the two groups is like the blind and deaf, and the one who sees and hears; are they equal in likeness? Will you not remember?

WHAT IS THE PRESCRIPTION TO STOP THE MIND?

To transcend the mind it is helpful to reduce sensory perceptions and transmissions. Silence at all levels is necessary. These preliminary steps are needed to lose the idea of your identity. To be fully alert with all your senses and other faculties is necessary for earthly survival and progress. Yet the reverse state is needed to touch higher zones of spiritual reality.

There is a natural human drive to touch limits of safety and the usual boundaries in life. We desire to go past limitations. The soul is external and boundless.

However, in our world today, with its large human population and long life expectation, mental illness is prevalent and this is a great distraction from the natural drive towards higher intelligence and transcendence in consciousness. Some people might find it difficult or even frightening to reach a point of transcendence.

A healthy mind is naturally occupied in the beneficial pursuit of good health and anything that provides a better understanding of the world of dualities. We naturally desire a silent mind and pure presence without too much outer or inner noise or distraction. Sleep requires some preparation: silence, darkness, comfortable dress and a good mattress. Similarly, quieting the mind also requires preparation: a relaxed and pleasant environment to practice inner silence and tranquillity. Pleasant thoughts, chanting, soothing sounds and visualizations may also help.

> *Human beings are naturally driven to be physically, mentally and emotionally relaxed as a prelude to still the mind and transcend all thoughts.*

What is the prescription to stop the mind?

48:4 It is He who sent down the tranquillity into the hearts of the believers, that they might add faith to their faith – to Allah belong the hosts of the heavens and the earth; Allah is All-Knowing, All-Wise.

WHAT ROLE DOES RELIGION PLAY IN AWAKENING AND ILLUMINATION?

At different times in different parts of the world religion brought about considerable growth in consciousness amongst different people.

For the last 3000 years or so, the issue of faith, belief, and the nature of life after death have preoccupied many people. As such, religions have helped many people to understand the meaning of responsibility and accountability for their intentions and actions. It has been central in bringing about higher awareness, respect for other living beings and encouraging service and generosity to others.

The wonderful world that we live in now and the fact that most humans everywhere share many values, like kindness and generosity, while also mutually condemning acts such as spitefulness, meanness and destructiveness, are the results of the previous religious values and the rise in intelligence. We should however not forget that there has also been crimes and injustices, committed individually or collectively in the name of religion.

The most significant role of religions was building communities and nations. Even though the world has become increasingly secular, religion still plays a role in improving quality of life and values. Good behaviour and exhibiting virtues such as honesty and integrity are no longer ascribed to any religion, but have become respected public behaviour.

> *The idea of a Supreme Power that we cannot influence or manipulate brings about humility and basic equality amongst people.*

What role does religion play in awakening and illumination?

Religions have played a powerful role in establishing the world we are living in today. Religion still nourishes many aspects of human life. Having faith and believing in accountability for one's actions are helpful traits to experience higher consciousness.

3:19 The true religion with Allah is Islam. Those who were given the Book were not at variance except after the knowledge came to them, being insolent one to another. And whoso disbelieves in Allah's signs. Allah is swift at the reckoning.

39:22 Consider therefore where stands one whose breast Allah spreads open to Islam. He is surely walking in the light of his Lord. But alas for the hard of heart for abandoning the remembrance of Allah! These are in flagrant error.

37:84 When he came unto his Lord with a pure heart.

How Can We Live in the Moment Fully?

Time emerges from that mysterious Source of timelessness; infinite and boundless. Since time emerges from eternity, it has a divine touch and power. The amount of time we are allotted is bracketed between birth and death and to touch timelessness you need intelligence, grace and prayers.

Time is the biggest illusion that is necessary for life to continue on earth. Our connection with the timeless state is through time, hence time becomes the most valuable thing that we have as it links the absolute (quantum state) with the relative (space-time domain).

Pathways to the Garden

The divine light of life within you transmits its nature of eternity and timelessness through your own soul.

Human experience is within space and time. Sometimes we experience time as very slow, whilst at other times we experience it as moving fast, especially during pleasant and joyful states. We are anxious because time is always ticking away, it can never return.

> *To transcend time requires a shift in consciousness from being in the flow of time to being at the Source of time.*

Once we know the truth of our own soul, that it is timeless, the anxiety caused by the ticking clock will stop. Our bodies, minds, and day to day biography change with time, but the soul is constant and eternal.

Our connection with the eternal God is through time. Our spirit or soul is in the zone of time, but will also continue beyond time. The human experience of a limited lifespan on earth is a sample of eternal life as transmitted by the divine creator of all. Because our soul is eternal, we need have no fear about the end of time.

How can we live in the moment fully?

103:1 By time,

103:2 most surely man is in loss,

103:3 All save those who believe, Who do righteous deeds, Who enjoin truth upon one another, Who enjoin patience upon one another.

55:29 All in the heavens and earth beseech Him; He is ever engaged upon some matter.

6:60 It is He who recalls you by night, and He knows what you work by day; then He raises you up therein, that a stated term may be determined; then unto Him shall you return, then He will tell you of what you have been doing.

How Can One Attain Pure Awareness?

Awareness follows specific patterns. You can be aware that you are concerned, that you heard something, or that you are looking at something. But subtler awarenesses can also arise, a higher witnessing of a state, an awareness of a specific awareness. Then you are more aware of the meaning than the specific form. Aggression becomes more powerful than the aggressor.

We are often naturally aware of many things simultaneously with varying degrees of focus. Physical or sensory awareness leads to subtler interpretations until it becomes pure awareness, and that is what leads to true spiritual boundlessness.

Awareness of awareness takes one out of the specific narrative of consciousness. Don't deny the story, but go beyond its details, to its source of pure energy. There one finds different streams of energies which connect, interact, mingle and move. The so-called you is a colour that emerges from the light of consciousness, capturing these movements of shadows and making a movie out of it, producing a personal biography as virtual reality. In your life you are perpetually erasing and editing episodes of awareness, with slight variations each time.

> *When awareness is not focusing on any specific entity or idea, then it is pure awareness; a light without any shadows.*

Awareness itself is almost like a blank slate: nothing has been inscribed on it yet. Once you have reached a subtler state of non-inscribing, of not focusing on any specific entity or idea emerging in the field of consciousness, you have reached awareness of awareness, or pure awareness.

How can one attain pure awareness?

13:28 Those who have faith and whose hearts find peace in the remembrance of Allah – truly it is in the remembrance of Allah that hearts find peace.

29:51 Was it not enough for them that We sent down the Book on you to be recited to them? In this is a mercy and a remembrance to a people who have faith.

40:54 as a guidance and a reminder for those who were endowed with the kernel.

50:8 An eye-opener is this, and a remembrance to every servant turn in repentance.

How can we be prepared, ready and cheerful about death?

Of all human experiences, birth and death are the most natural. Birth is the emergence from boundless eternity to experience the limitations of space and time. Death is the return to eternity and implies the loss of our biographies and physical experiences. In deep dreamless sleep, when you lose the ego-self temporarily, you are at the doorway of death.

Any living thing that is born will die. Any idea or emotion that is born will also die. Birth and death are concomitant. The forces and powers that cause death are there before birth.

Practice death by losing your conscious identity in order to transcend the mental illusion of 'entity'. We put stories together in our heads about our identities and we need to take them apart. Rather weave stories in your mind to create identities and then take them apart to replace them with new narratives.

> *Death is merely a shift in consciousness from duality to cosmic unity.*

We are merely custodians or hosts of the soul. If the soul is happy, provided with a pleasant environment and taken care of, it will continue for a while before returning to the spirit domain. Like a flame it appears from the unseen and then disappears again.

How can we be prepared, ready and cheerful about death?

89:27 O self at peace!

89:28 Return to your Lord, Well pleased, well pleasing,

2:156 Those who say, when afflicted with a calamity, 'We belong to Allah and to Him we shall return'.

3:185 Every self will taste death and you will be paid in full only on the Day of Resurrection. Whoever is kept away from the Fire and admitted to the Garden will have triumphed. And this present life is but the rapture of delusion.

WHAT DOES IT MEAN TO DIE BEFORE YOU DIE?

Human life is experienced within space and time and can be happy or miserable, or somewhere in between. Life itself is not touched by any external state, it is perfect when it emerges within space and time.

To practice death before physical death implies conscious and wilful absence of all awareness of the pattern of life's experiences to which we have become accustomed. It means leaving the field of energy of conditioned consciousness. Give up all thoughts, desires or ambitions before physical death removes all of these illusions. Do it by grace of higher intelligence within you. Lose the ego-self and be the soul or spirit who you truly and eternally are.

It is a grace to step aside from the power of the importance we have assigned to a relationship, a career, or any hope or desire. Extinguish the flame of all emotions like fears, sorrow, anxiety and jealousy.

> *Stop all physical, mental and emotional connections whilst conscious to lose any discernible awareness.*

What does it mean to die before you die?

29:64 This present life is nothing but frivolity and amusement. But the Abode of the Hereafter is the real life, if only they knew!

2:109 Many of the followers of the Book wish that they could turn you back into unbelievers after your faith, out of envy from themselves, after the truth has be- come manifest to them; but pardon and forgive, till Allah brings His command; surely Allah has power over all things.

29:57 Every self shall taste death and then to Us you shall revert.

How does one take reference from the Higher without a visible outer authority?

The way to light is to avoid darkness. To access higher consciousness the first step is to stop being governed by the shadows of the lower ego-self. The key is less distraction.

A trustworthy and supportive human being can be useful as counsel or reference and can act as an excellent enabling tool. But for a mature person it is not necessary anymore to have a specific teacher. You are here climbing a ladder to higher knowledge and consciousness and anything that helps you can lift you onto the next rung of that ladder.

If you are in the present moment and observant you may learn from anything in your natural environment, even animals and plants. You may learn from silence or the buzz of a bee. Be open to the hints around you and you may benefit from subtle signs, as well as profound or powerful impacts. Anything that takes you out of the mundane to the higher levels of consciousness can act as a teacher.

> *Higher consciousness implies constancy and durability, and any reliable reference we seek is from a higher state of consciousness.*

Taking reference includes looking at numerous beams of consciousness. When you have pain in your finger, your reference is the finger itself and ways to reduce the pain. We are consciously and intuitively driven to reduce pain and avoid life-threatening situations.

How does one take reference from the Higher without a visible outer authority?

Higher on the ladder of consciousness there are fewer distractions and illusions in your mind. Your focus is on the Highest and therefore it is narrow and restricted. Most people generally consider anything that reduces the power of self-ego as undesirable. When, by effort and grace, you are relieved from the darkness of the lower self, the light of the soul or spirit within your own heart guides you faithfully and efficiently.

21:107 And We have not sent you but as a mercy to the worlds.

39:29 Allah strikes a parable: a man shared by partners at loggerheads, and a man belonging wholly to another man – can the two be equal in likeness? Allah be praised! In truth, most of them are ignorant.

26:78 He is Who created me, and He is Who guides me;

WHAT IS THE ROLE OF FEAR AND HOPE IN AWAKENING?

Most emotions are balanced between two extremes. Fear and hope are usually the most dominant. We fear suffering and we hope to be in a healthy, pleasant state. We fear loss and hope for the ultimate gain, which is eternal life.

Early in life, when personal consciousness is being built up, fear works more effectively than hope; whereas later on, with growth and maturity, it is hope that drives one along more than fear.

In the past the collective consciousness had been dominated by fear, whereas today hope plays a more significant role. This can be attributed to the rise in consciousness and intelligence.

Fear and hope drive us effectively away from darkness and ignorance to divine light. When we were evolving as animals, fear had been the main driving factor, but in the last few generations hope and courage started dominating.

There is a natural balance between fear and hope, but with awakening to higher consciousness we are distracted less by the shadowy ego-self and guided more by the light of our soul until we experience pure presence that transcends most emotions.

> *Life is experienced within dualities as it emerges from higher consciousness to this conditioned state.*

What is the role of fear and hope in awakening?

32:16 Their sides shun their couches as they call on their Lord in fear and hope; and they expend of that We have provided them.

WHAT IS THE ROLE OF KNOWLEDGE IN AWAKENING?

Awakening is the result of connections that unify the light of the known with the darkness of ignorance. Power appear in numerous beams or strands, and knowledge is one of them. Knowledge is the connector, it links cause and effect to reveal oneness and awakening. Knowledge is a great unifying quality that occurs with the right conditions and readiness.

A ten year old child may not understand the reasoning and actions of a twenty year old. Hence, some knowledge is shareable, but some of it is not.

The more knowledge you have, the more empowered you feel. That is why you are driven to discover a secret that someone is keeping from you. Keeping knowledge from people is generally considered unfair. Souls are the same and thus the ego-selves are to be treated with equity and fairness. Your soul is in a state of total contentment and if you touch that state when your desire to know will abate. The presence is enough.

Yet a time may also come that you have acquired so much knowledge that it impedes involvement in action. Doubt can occur due to little knowledge or excess of it.

> *Humans are driven towards greater knowledge, which brings greater power, ultimately leading towards awakening.*

In the realm of duality, it is natural to pursue knowledge, but when you are touching the zone of higher consciousness, you know that whatever knowledge is required will be given at the time when it is actually needed. Once you know, through transcendence, that what you really need to know to maintain

What is the role of knowledge in awakening?

balance, equanimity and presence, will come to you at the time that you need it, then you no longer hanker after knowledge. The presence will guide you.

17:80 And say: 'My Lord, lead me in with a just ingoing, and lead me out with a just outgoing; grant me authority from Thee, to help me.'

29:69 But those who exerted themselves in Our cause – these We shall guide to Our ways. and Allah is assuredly with the righteous.

WHAT IS THE IMPORTANCE OF BALANCE AND HOW DO WE ATTAIN IT?

Human beings are naturally driven to be well, at ease, and to reflect upon what they observe and experience. Humanity lies between the beginning of life and the state of awakening to the Truth after death. Therefore it is our duty to maintain this middle-path – between birth and death, between non-consciousness and higher consciousness, and between dualities and attributes. To be kind but not indulgent. To be firm but not harsh. To be considerate but not indifferent.

Whatever we experience has a beginning and an end. The beginning has within it promises, hopes, expectations, and the end may be sweet, like the contentment at the end of a good meal, or it may be laced with sorrow. To be balanced in the middle enables us to see both extreme ends with ease. If we are in the middle we gain a better perspective and can see and evaluate the situation better.

Balance has no meaning when you are no longer within conditioned consciousness; it is meaningless with pure consciousness.

> *The zone of duality requires us to maintain balance between the two attributes.*

The biggest gift in life is the absence of the ego-self that maintains the illusion of being a doer. Movement of time provides new events, some of which we engage with and others we just witness.

Balance is the healthy state to be in with respect to the zone of duality that we live in during our journey on earth. The soul or spirit is beyond human values and understanding.

What is the importance of balance and how do we attain it?

55:9 Weigh with justice and do not fall short in the balance.

7:56 Do not corrupt the land once it has been set right. Call upon Him in fear and in hope, for the mercy of Allah is within reach of the righteous.

57:25 We sent Our messengers with clear signs, the Scripture and the Balance, so that people could uphold justice: We also sent iron, with its mighty strength and many uses for mankind, so that Allah could mark out those who would help Him and His messengers though they cannot see Him. Truly Allah is Powerful, Almighty.

WHAT ARE THE QUALITIES OF THE 'MIDDLE PEOPLE'?

The state of the 'Middle people' is suspended between the highest and lowest levels of consciousness. It can be referred to as temporary conditioned consciousness.

Human kind is held within a life force that provides the possibilities between the highest level of eternal consciousness and limited awareness and sentience. We cannot light a fire anywhere; it has prerequisite conditions, and to maintain it requires a further set of conditions. For a flame to occur you need appropriate conditions, so an evolutionary process was required for the light of the soul to manifest on earth through humankind.

We experience life within the field of dualities: beginnings and ends, accept and reject, good and bad, etc. Our consciousness encompasses the two extremes and is mostly in the middle of these two extremes. Even when we are breathing, more time is spent between inhaling and exhaling. When we sleep, we are in another zone of consciousness, and when we are awake, it is considered the normal conditioned consciousness with its numerous strands of modes and moods.

To be in the middle is the wisest and most intelligent state for our life on earth.

> *Human nature is between timeless, boundless consciousness and conditioned consciousness. We are in the middle between the ever-changing and the perfect constant state.*

What are the qualities of the 'middle people'?

9:71 The believers, male and female, are friends of one another. They command to virtue and forbid vice. They perform the prayers and pay the alms, and they obey Allah and His Messenger. These, Allah shall show them mercy. Allah is Almighty, All-Wise.

73:8 And remember the name of your Lord, And devote yourself to Him, in consummate devotion.

39:18 who listen to what is said and follow what is best. These are the ones Allah has guided; these are the people of the kernel.

WHAT DOES IT MEAN TO EMPTY OUR MIND AND PURIFY OUR HEART?

We cannot interact in this world without judgement, but suffering and darkness prevails when you let your past shadows stay alive within you. Times have changed, you have changed, and yet you carry on with the same fixed opinions you had. Trouble naturally follows.

Good life experiences are due to appropriate interactions, balance and moving on to other stimuli and responses. Life emerges from the past and becomes the present before the future. An endless flow in time by grace of eternity. The ego-self remains in transit and the soul ever constant.

Emptying out implies not carrying the burden of any past experiences that brings about fears, anxieties and other concerns. It also implies trusting, being present in the moment, including the flow of grace that will ensure that the future will always be better. That is the foundation of hope and trust for uplifting consciousness and intelligence by grace.

> *Much suffering and confusion is due to competing and conflicting thoughts and emotions. Emptying out is a necessary state for a healthier presence.*

What does it mean to empty our mind and purify our heart?

94:7 When your work is done, turn to devotion.

22:46 What, have they not journeyed in the land so that they have hearts to understand with or ears to hear with? It is not the eyes that are blind, but blind are the hearts that turn away within the breasts.

9:125 As for those with sickness in their hearts, it shall increase them in pollution, adding to their pollution, and they shall die as unbelievers.

83:14 No indeed! Their hearts are encrusted with what they have done.

3:7 It is He Who sent down the Book upon you. In it are verses precise in meaning, these are the very heart of the Book. Others are ambiguous. Those in whose heart is waywardness pursue what is ambiguous therein, seeking discord and seeking to unravel its interpretation. But none knows its interpretation save Allah, while those deeply rooted in knowledge say: 'We believe in it. All is from our Lord.' Yet none remembers save those possessed of the kernel.

WHY ARE WE DRIVEN TOWARDS ACHIEVEMENT AND SUCCESS?

The human desire to succeed and achieve excellence reflects the spiritual perfection of the soul itself. I'm alive due to the soul, even though I may not know it or admit it. Consciousness of life within us drives us towards the source of life itself — where higher consciousness is constant, timeless and not confined to space.

The soul is in a state beyond achievement; it is in total unison and submission to eternal reality itself, or God. Therefore its shadow, the so-called 'I', carries that memory and attempts to reach excellence, but if it gets there it is only temporary, because it is confined to space and time. The so-called 'I', which is energized by the eternal spirit, will always aspire to achieve that permanent state.

Achievement or success is like the end of a chapter of a story or an event. Here it is, I've done it. We want to achieve something to end a chapter or a sentence in our stories.

We desire success because we experience an ever-changing state in consciousness as we grow towards a higher one, so it is a work in progress; it is not a fixed state. We are propelled into this unknown with the boundless and eternal light. Through some effort and participation, we will internalise and embrace the rise in consciousness until we realise the truth: that the soul has been present from the beginning.

> *In our earthly conditioned consciousness we go through loops of beginnings and ends, desiring success and shunning failure; all of which may prepare us for the achievement of divine presence as a soul – the source of all consciousness.*

Why are we driven towards achievement and success?

Our life on earth is a participative endeavour, through intelligence and efforts, towards higher states of consciousness. It is part of the rise in consciousness that occasionally makes us want to be acknowledged as doers.

53:42 and to your Lord is the final destination.

84:6 you humans, toiling laboriously towards your Lord, will meet Him:

4:48 Allah forgives not that aught should be with Him associated; less than that He forgives to whomsoever He will. Whoso associates with Allah anything, has indeed forged a mighty misdeed.

WHAT IS THE TRUTH ABOUT KARMA?

In the Hindu tradition Karma is highly developed and defined from numerous angles, but in a broader and universal sense we can benefit by understanding the basic truth of karma.

Karma is action and reaction, always together and inseparable. Nothing is missed, everything is in balance. Therefore, whatever you think, intend, or do, will have a repercussion, not necessarily as intended or hoped for. Every action comes with a pattern that will begin to unfold, which we call reaction or outcome. Whatever you do, you will also be exposed to its outcome, to the reaction, and you cannot escape that. Therefore, before you do anything, you must review the intention, the correctness, appropriateness and relevance of your action. Only then you might be in balance. If you don't examine your intentions, you will suffer from that imbalance, and that is called bad karma.

For future karmic consequences, be clear about what your intentions and actions are and its possible effects on the community, or nature itself, like climate change. The rise of consciousness amongst human beings regarding our carbon footprint and our disturbance of the balance in nature is an indicator of rising caution about karma.

> *In many cultures, the link between cause and effect has been useful to improve people's conduct and their awareness of intention and action.*

What is the truth about karma?

30:8 Have they not pondered within themselves? Allah did not create the heavens and earth, and what lies between, except in truth, and for a stated term. And yet many there are who disavow the encounter with their Lord.

4:123 It is not your fancies, nor the fancies of the People of the Book. Whosoever does evil shall be recompensed for it, and will not find for him, apart from Allah, a friend or helper.

WHAT IS WAHM AND KHAYAL?

Human conditioning is initiated by the illusion of this so-called reality. Khayal is the important imaginal faculty for human because it provides a realistic illusion of what we consider to be real. It has the colour, flavour and characteristics of something that is durable, whereas in reality, it is not. For example, I have the illusion that my father is the provider of our sustenance. He is certainly a visible actor in that domain, but there are many other factors that enable him to act as such. It is the 'imaginal' that bestows this role upon him, but I say that he is the source of livelihood.

The imaginal or khayal is what makes us human beings and it helps us to view our earthly ever-changing experiences as real. What reinforces this so-called reality, is wahm: the value that we attach to situations and events. I consider my employment as a crucial reason for my wellbeing, therefore if I lose it, I am upset and may even become physically ill. I have ascribed a disproportionate value to a situation that is changeable by its very nature. We human beings interact and share life's experience on earth due to the imaginal and the value we attach to situations. What we are truly obsessed with is life itself, boundless and eternal. That is the ultimate treasure.

If we can practice to die and remove these lenses, then our lives may be more enriched. This is one of the meanings of to die before you die.

> *Whatever we call reality has a touch of what is real and constant. But our so-called realities are ever-changing, like a shadow – this is khayal. The values that we give to certain things or emotions is called wahm.*

3:54 They schemed but Allah also schemed;
Allah is the Best of Schemers.

20:66 He said: 'No, you cast first.' And it was as if their ropes and staffs appeared to him, through their sorcery, to be swiftly moving.

WHAT IS FANA AND BAQA?

There are a few dozen Sufi terms that correlate with the rise of certain Sufi trends, which, over time, became popular. Fana and Baqa are two of them, even though they were not used throughout Muslim history.

A certain Sufi path would embrace a few of these terms at a point in time and it would become not just fashionable, but part of their day-to-day language. The Chishti movement played a big role in bringing higher knowledge to the Muslims, and they based a considerable amount of discourse around the concepts of Fana and Baqa.

Fana means to be subject to time, beginnings and endings, that which is short-lived. Baqa refers to the eternal, that which is ever there – the divine light and life itself.

We are all seekers of the long-lived, of continuity, without denying the short-lived. For example, we cannot deny hunger and suffering. We have to address the short-lived, do what we have to do about it, while at the same time we must also calibrate with the everlasting.

> *Anything that has a beginning will have an end – Fana.*

With wisdom we should reduce our reliance on specific identities and seek qualities and virtues that lead us out of the darkness of the ego-self to the light of the soul. When the sugar has melted it no longer exists as an entity on its own. Yet the sugar hasn't died, but has given itself up into the syrup to make something sweet.

What is the secret of Baqa? There is only Baqa – durable, boundless and timeless in Reality.

Human consciousness and awareness of beginnings and ends, especially death, emerge from a higher zone of consciousness that is not subject to space-time limitations. The real me, my ruh or my soul, is ever living, but the human 'me' experiences the constant drift towards death and liberation from uncertainty.

With appropriate mental adjustment and practices we may emerge to live by the knowledge and the essence of the soul, which is ever-living. But we will still experience death as separation of body and mind from our soul. When someone says that our real essence is a secret, the implication is that it is not obvious but hidden, and cannot be described or measured. In fact our soul announces itself through every aspect of our lives. We are obsessed by it.

> *Anything that exists, known and unknown, emanates from the source of what is eternally there – Baqa.*

28:88 And call not upon another Allah with Allah; there is no Allah but He. All things perish, except His Face. His is the Judgment, and unto Him you shall be returned.

88:20 how the earth is spread out?

88:21 Therefore do remind, for you are only a reminder.

12:21 The man who bought him, from Egypt, said to his wife: 'Treat him hospitably, for he might be of use to us, or else we might adopt him as a son.' Thus did We establish Joseph firmly on earth, in order that We might teach him the interpretation of reports. Allah's decree will prevail, but most people do not know.

What is Tawakkul?

The root meaning of Tawakkul is to rely upon; its foundation is to connect. That is the fabric of existence: everything is interconnected. A simple physical act, like walking or lifting a finger, relies on our limbs being in working order and the nerves being connected to our brain.

Ultimately the aim is to depend entirely upon the Source of life itself, which has designed and created all the patterns and pathways of our experiences. Tawakkul implies our hopes will lead to contentment.

Trust is an issue of reliance or dependency on both the seen and unseen powers. Tawakkul does not preclude doing what you can to reach a desirable objective, but throughout this process you place your trust in God.

Tawakkul develops in stages. It grows with intellect and reason. The first cognisance of it is between a baby and a mother, when an early trust is established.

Participative reliance or trust is the root of intelligence. Without trust, we would not be able to participate in normal day to day functions. When we sleep, we trust that we will rest and wake up the next day with vigour and energy. A more subtle level of trust in the evolution of our consciousness is that good deeds will beget goodness.

> *Trust is reliance on the One and dependence on the Divine.*

Our consciousness expands from duality to its unitive source. Human life is to practice the rise of intelligence to that unitive source, which requires trust in that evolution. It is only the identification of the so-called 'I' with its biography of beginnings and ends, with all its ups and downs, which prevents it from being constantly delighted by the present moment.

We live in a zone of uncertainty; all we can be sure of is our earthly existence will change and eventually end. But if we have faith and trust we will believe that this end will be the beginning of eternal life. It is Tawakkul that will guide us to a Paradise without seasons.

33:3 *Put your trust in Allah – let Allah suffice as worthy of all trust.*

49:7 *Know that the Messenger of Allah is among you; had he heeded your words in many a matter, you would have suffered hardship. But Allah has endeared faith to you and adorned it in your hearts, and made unbelief, depravity and mutiny hateful to you. These are rightly guided:*

65:3 *and shall provide for him from where he never imagined. Whoso places his trust in Allah, Allah shall suffice him. Allah enforces what He commands. For all things Allah has set a measure.*

WHAT IS THE REASON AND PURPOSE OF WORSHIP?

The purpose of worship is to raise your consciousness to a higher level so that you can envision the Divine side as well as the human. It begins with respect, admiration, adoring the Divine, a desire to be close, to love until you find yourself obsessed with worship. This is the path to experience cosmic oneness.

Human nature is obsessive. According to its level of consciousness, anything that has been touched by life, anything that is alive, is obsessed by life itself. Living things want to contain life and will defend itself to maintain the life within it.

It is natural for each one of us to be enthusiastic and driven to the ultimate point of utter obsession with the perfection that life exudes. We are driven to do what we can in the best possible way. But we're also allowed to experiment and make mistakes, hopefully not irretrievable, so that next time we are more focused, less distracted, more aware of what we're doing and more worshipful. It's all about perfecting worship and improving the quality and subtleness of our worship. We may begin with some limitations due to past experiences and distractions and with grace attain focus, perfect stillness and presence.

> *Obsession is the doorway to Oneness.*

What is the reason and purpose of worship?

13:28 Those who have faith and whose hearts find peace in the remembrance of Allah – truly it is in the remembrance of Allah that hearts find peace.

70:23 who are constantly at prayer.

39:9 Or is he who is obedient in the watches of the night, bowing himself and standing, he being afraid of the world to come and hoping for the mercy of his Lord? Say: 'Are they equal – those who know and those who know not?' Only men possessed of the kernel remember.

WHAT ARE THE PITFALLS ON THE PATH TOWARDS ONENESS?

Anything other than Oneness implies duality, plurality and multiplicity and the illusion of separation from the origin of Oneness, which encompasses everything at all times.

We emerged from Oneness and we are on our way back to Oneness. Our souls are exposed to illusory experiences in a zone of conditioned consciousness. Therefore, as humans our normal state is duality with an inner drive towards our origin, which is Tawhid (unity or oneness); where there is no notion of duality or otherness; perpetual oneness prevails.

When we are born, a natural progression of dualities are experienced. We are attracted to something, or repulsed by it; we want something, or we don't want it; until we realise that both the attraction and the repulsion emanate from the same source. At this point we are moving towards a higher intelligence beyond duality.

Human life is lived almost entirely within duality, but with reflection, deep silence, or meditation, we realise that all of these states emerge from the same source. At this point our rejection or acceptance of things or situations becomes less obsessive. What we don't like now may be the best thing for us tomorrow. What we desire might be a catastrophe. What we consider to be medicine can be poison, or vice versa. Life on earth is based on dualities, and the confusion this state causes is the main obstacle to witnessing oneness.

> *For most of our life we are driven by the soul within dualities and the illusion of the ego-self as an independent entity.*

What are the pitfalls on the path towards Oneness?

You are at the point of oneness when there is no choice or confusion of duality, insecurity, fears or sorrow. There is deep contentment and joy within the present moment.

Whilst we are in duality, we are eager to experience this state of oneness and be established in it with no further ambitions, fears and concerns.

Another common pitfall in the quest for Oneness lies in the quest to acquire virtuous qualities, such as accountability, generosity, kindness and helpfulness, which, in themselves are admirable. Virtue is always admirable, but when we perceive ourselves as performing these acts and becoming a virtuous person, we become trapped in the snare of self-importance. The feeling of piety and virtuosity can be a challenging obstacle.

3:66 Consider. It was you who argued about a matter of which you have knowledge. Why then do you argue about a matter of which you have no knowledge? Allah knows and you do not know.

28:55 When they hear idle talk, they turn away from it and say, 'We have our deeds, and you your deeds. Peace be upon you! We desire not the ignorant.'

7:3 Follow what has been sent down to you from your Lord and follow not, apart from Him, any other guardians. Little do you remember!

12:53 I do not declare my soul innocent: the soul ever urges to evil, except when my Lord shows mercy. My Lord is All-Forgiving, Compassionate to each.'

WHAT DOES IT MEAN TO WITNESS PERFECTION?

We often describe perfection with reference to our expectations and objectives. When there is a perfect fit or greater benefit. But there is also perfection in the web of connections that leads to failure and disappointment. There is a perfection in whatever happens even though it is not what is desired or hoped for. To see a situation as perfect irrespective of it being a success or a failure requires total neutrality and openness; not easy when there is a personal desire or involvement.

Whatever we experience emanates from a Source of higher consciousness beyond the limitations of space and time and as such it is ever perfect. We, living in duality, only consider something as perfect if it is in accordance with what we are driven to achieve. But while there is perfection in that drive, there is also perfection in failure, or in chaos. If you look at it on its own, you find that it has its own cosmology of perfection.

Every moment carries a beam of perfection with it, but after it interacts with physical realities, human values and expectations, it can be accepted or rejected.

In essence whatever exists and the destiny of everything is ever perfect. It is with human objectives and projects in mind that definitions of imperfection, difficulties, disharmony and other judgments arise. As things are in themselves, there is a natural flow of connection or disconnection, and beginnings and endings.

> *Whatever has been touched by the divine Source carries the quality of perfection.*

The human soul or spirit is in a zone beyond our conditioned consciousness and is ever-perfect in its state of eternal boundlessness and harmony. Due to that spirit within us, we aspire for harmonious flow and goodness at all times, so we can always be in the state of witnessing perfection.

What does it mean to witness perfection?

67:3 Who created the seven heavens one above another; you see no incongruity in the creation of the Beneficent Allah; then look again, can you see any disorder?

2:115 And to Allah belongs the east and the west. So wherever you turn, there is the Face of Allah. Allah is All-Encompassing and Knowing.

51:50 Therefore flee unto Allah! I am a clear warner from Him to you.

What Is Our Ultimate Destiny?

The cosmic mystery of eternal life and its boundlessness contains the seeds of anything and everything known and unknown. The experience of life is introduced slowly, beginning in the womb and continuing throughout life, transcending space and time to eternity.

Optimism is an important factor in a healthy drive towards a good destiny. It is to believe that things will always be better in the sense of durability and expansion of consciousness. It is to look forward to escaping the prison of time and space.

Our ultimate destiny is being inseparable from boundless and eternal light. In the meantime we experience more limited horizons of consciousness. The quest becomes complete with the total loss of personal identity and separation from the illusion of separation from Divine Grace.

Our perfect destiny is being prepared by our intentions and actions until our identity is at one with cosmic Unity from which the entire cosmos had emerged. With a clear mind and a pure heart and constantly being present in the moment with honesty, courage and accountability, the final destiny will acknowledge our commitment and drive to unify with the light of oneness.

> *Our desired destiny is to be at one with the state of joyful Oneness that permeates all.*

What is our ultimate destiny?

53:42 and to your Lord is the final destination.

55:27 'And there remains the Face of your Lord, Majestic and Noble.'

9:51 Say: 'Naught shall visit us but what Allah has prescribed for us; He is our Protector; in Allah let the believers put all their trust.'

Milton Keynes UK
Ingram Content Group UK Ltd.
UKHW042005240924
448733UK00005B/260